Summary Bundle: Leadership & Success | Readtrepreneur Publishing: Includes Summary of Leaders Eat Last & Summary of Lean In

By: Simon Sinek

Proudly Brought to you by:

Legal & Disclaimer

The information contained in this book is not designed to replace or take the place of any form of medicine or professional medical advice. The information in this book has been provided for educational and entertainment purposes only.

The information contained in this book has been compiled from sources deemed reliable, and it is accurate to the best of the Author's knowledge; however, the Author cannot guarantee its accuracy and validity and cannot be held liable for any errors or omissions. Changes are periodically made to this book. You must consult your doctor or get professional medical advice before using any of the suggested remedies, techniques, or information in this book. Images used in this book is not the same as of that of the actual book. This is a totally separate and different entity from that of the original book titled: *Leaders Eat Last"*.

Upon using the information contained in this book, you agree to hold harmless the Author from and against any damages, costs, and expenses, including any legal fees potentially resulting from the application of any of the information provided by this guide. This disclaimer applies to any damages or injury caused by the use and application, whether directly or indirectly, of any advice or information presented, whether for breach of contract, tort, negligence, personal injury, criminal intent, or under any other cause of action.

Table of Contents

The Book at a Glance

It's only when each one of us strives to develop leadership qualities that we can collaborate towards a cause bigger than ourselves: the sustainability of mankind's survival. Today, we are a self-destructive society due to overabundance, and we have become stagnant in our progress as a species. Good leaders must steer us through the right course so that we may progress, but this doesn't mean that we sit and wait for someone to come and redeem us: we have to take charge ourselves.

Simon Sinek retraces our roots as hunters and gatherers in order to demonstrate how true leaders perform in the modern world. He provides an in-depth take on human physiology to exhibit how we have always been built to work together. Endorphins, dopamine, serotonin, and oxytocin: these chemicals serve as powerful forces that drive man towards cooperation and survival. He states that, like our primitive selves, we are still dependent on them.

With the right balance of these chemicals, we can form strong organizations built on cooperation, trust, love, and loyalty. To demonstrate this, Sinek provides examples of real individuals and organizations that have both failed and succeeded throughout history, clarifying the difference between groups who have unhealthy cultures of self-preservation versus those who've built strong Circles of Safety that prioritize the collective. He sheds light on the sins of the past and how we transformed ourselves into a society of dehumanization and abstraction. Fortunately, we can adopt values that will help us rise from this slump in the form of five rules: keeping it real, keeping it manageable, meeting the people we help, giving them time and not just money, and being patient.

We have to look back to a time when enough was enough in order to live within our means today and onwards to the future. Sinek educates us on "destructive abundance" and the leadership lessons we have to learn so we could breed good cultures and thus, good leaders – all while understanding the true nature of power, recognizing the significance of integrity, and considering humans not as numbers but as the people they are. Our self-centeredness threatens these values as we have become a society of addicts, enslaved by the instantaneous, feel-good dopamine high from addictive substances and technological distractions.

Sinek likens this modern addiction to substance abuse itself. We cannot be cured standing alone. It is only through sharing the struggle with others that we can rise above it. And the strongest motivation we have towards our own betterment is a cause bigger than ourselves: a purpose that serves the entire community. Sinek recognizes that when a goal is beyond our resources but within our capabilities, we will strive to achieve it no matter what. Our goal now is to make sure mankind lives today and survives tomorrow, leaving a legacy that will keep the global community strong for generations to come. We need leaders to guide us through this path. But no matter how relevant hierarchy is to maintaining order, Sinek tells us that it's not up to a chosen few to solve the problems of the modern world. *Leaders Eat Last* concludes with its most significant war cry: we must all act like the leaders we dream to follow.

Foreword

Modern institutions and training programs teach us that it's important to nurture managerial skills, failing to recognize that it's much more significant to train effective leaders. This is the paradigm that *Leaders Eat Last* aims to shift. Simon Sinek emphasizes that the success of any organization depends on leadership excellence as a whole, not just the leader's critical thinking abilities or decision-making prowess. This is exactly why he uses the United States Marine Corps as a best example, given that this branch of the U.S. military exhibits teamwork and shared values while being a model for interpersonal relationships. The connections within are so vital especially when the cost of a failed mission is fatal, and success is the only acceptable result.

The effective dynamics of the interpersonal connections within the Marine Corps are best displayed when the team gathers to eat. The juniors are served first and the seniors last, and the behavior isn't forced by any means. One principle is emphasized: true leaders place the interests of others above their own. Sinek provides an in-depth explanation of such human behaviors of true leaders that are beyond managerial.

FREE BONUSES

P.S. Is it okay if we overdeliver?

Here at Readtrepreneur Publishing, we believe in
overdelivering way beyond our reader's expectations. Is it
okay if we overdeliver?

Here's the deal, we're going to give you an extremely
condensed PDF summary of the book which you've just read
and much more...

What's the catch? We need to trust you... You see, we want
to overdeliver and in order for us to do that, we've to trust our
reader to keep this bonus a secret to themselves? Why?
Because we don't want people to be getting our exclusive
PDF summaries even without buying our books itself.
Unethical, right?

Ok. Are you ready?

Firstly, remember that your book is code: "**READ49**".

Next, visit this link: **http://bit.ly/exclusivepdfs**

Everything else will be self explanatory after you've visited:
http://bit.ly/exclusivepdfs.

We hope you'll enjoy our free bonuses as much as we enjoyed preparing it for you!

Our Need to Feel Safe

Protection from Above

Twenty-two men deep in enemy territory have captured a high-value target in Afghanistan. Captain Mike Drowley, nicknamed Johnny Bravo, instinctively took the risk of piloting his aircraft out of safety to be nearer his troops on the ground. He felt his men were in trouble before they even gave him the signal, and he was right. On August 16, 2002, he found himself in a combat situation for the first time. With limited resources and equipment, he had to rely on his capabilities to hit back at the enemy without harming his own men. When he ran out of ammo, Johnny Bravo skillfully led his wingman to lay down fire on cue. With all twenty-two men coming home alive, that night's mission had been a success.

The Value of Empathy

For Johnny Bravo, rewards from the top don't matter as much as service and self-sacrifice for others. And if he were to receive any recognition, he believes it will be for the greatest asset he brings to the table: empathy.

Even when not all of us can risk our life to save another, we are called upon to help others succeed and inspire them to do the same for us. This bond between people is the strongest invaluable foundation of an organization. Simon Sinek sheds light on this pattern found within the most successful teams – and like Johnny Bravo, he believes that the key is empathy.

Employees Are People Too

For Mike Merck and Ron Campbell, long-time employees at HayssenSandiacre, each workday had been all about starting at the bell and flipping machine switches; until Bob Chapman took over as CEO. Chapman acquired many companies that were on the brink of failure, breathing life back into them, all because he brought with him a willingness to listen. Ron told him how factory floor workers had to ask permission for the smallest freedoms. He felt that the company didn't trust them. Chapman made sure to change this system towards a more caring and trusting environment. It wasn't long until the workday felt like time spent with family, and the company thrived. The culture of trust and care that Chapman introduced inspired employees to work better, increasing the company's revenue from $55 million to $95 million after five years – all because the workers felt that they were valued.

We See What We Want to See

Chapman's eyes were opened to the harsh reality of the HayssenSandiacre workplace when he witnessed two employees suddenly changing from a good mood to a sullen demeanor once they were needed back on the floor. Before then, Chapman was only an excellent executive in the technical sense: good with numbers and making the hard decisions. After what he witnessed, he determined to improve the workplace environment in the aspect of care. His approach to the situation of HayssenSandiacre became his general model for managing his operation. He understood that the human mind constantly tries to find the most suitable situations to thrive and feel safe and that a true leader protects the organization from internal conflict much like how each part of the human body must cooperate in order for a person to live. This biological and anthropological view dictates that the right conditions must be met in order for members of a single body to work together – a pattern that can be observed in the most successful organizations.

Yet it seems that the modern world has not adopted this approach as much as needed. A majority of today's organizations are solely profit-driven with short-term goals in view, making work for employees obligatory and unsatisfactory. The impact that this has on society goes beyond work and into the home, as a dissatisfied worker may project negativity onto his family. Chapman's approach aims that each worker may come home feeling inspired and fulfilled.

The Awesome Responsibility

Chapman realized that, like the father of the bride entrusting his daughter to the groom, a leader of a company also becomes responsible for the welfare of its employees as they are handed over to the organization. When a leader acts like a parent and the company feels like a family, its members are loyal and proud of their identity. A high-performing company uses its money to help grow its people, which would enable the company to achieve true, long-term success – as opposed to an organization that puts money as its first priority. A leader who puts the people first only ever increases his credibility because excellent employee performance makes him look like a genius. Sinek realizes that such conditions may seem too idealistic, but it's undeniable that concrete examples do exist. The challenge now is for us to promulgate the importance of a culture of care within every organization; and in its absence, to care for one another like leaders should.

Belonging

From "Me" to "We"

When George finished his military training, he was confident and committed to his fellow United States Marines. With no threat of internal conflicts, they were ready for any outside dangers. As a unit, they were within the Circle of Safety.

With organizations, dangers come in the form of competition, obsoleteness, and meeting expectations. Among its people, there exists the threat of rejection, isolation, and the like. But these can be addressed if the people are enveloped by a sense of belongingness, a Circle of Safety, creating unity and teamwork. We can focus more on protecting the group from outside dangers when we don't have to protect ourselves from each other. Aside from the example of the Marines, people can draw inspiration from the Greek warrior society, the Spartans, who derived their strength mainly from the collective defense of their shields rather than individual spears or helms. It is the leader's responsibility to make sure everyone in the group pulls together in the same way. Furthermore, the leader determines how the Circle expands by "adopting new children" or taking on new members. Once the Circle has grown, he is in charge of overseeing the layers of management, making sure both his senior officers and the rest of the group are given equal consideration. This helps prevent unhealthy internal politics or self-preservation behaviors that threaten unity. When the Circle of Safety is strong, the group is trusting, collaborative, and innovative. And then, the twist: leaders need to feel safe, too. It's the responsibility of the members to openly communicate any concerns they may have regarding their leader's welfare.

Yeah, but...

Ken, a mid-ranking executive for a large bank, seemed happy with making a good living. But deep inside he wanted to quit and do something else entirely; except when he thought about his kids and the mortgage, he knew he didn't have a choice but to be a responsible man of the house even when it meant he had to work a job he didn't love.

Sinek recognizes the seemingly impossible challenge for companies to put their people first before the business, especially considering return on investment (ROI) , annual goals, competition, Wall Street, and all the external dangers to a company's success. Most of us, like Ken, see the reality of life and work the same way – that in order to satisfy a certain lifestyle, we must give up true happiness and fulfillment at work. But Sinek warns that job stability is a myth and that it demands a high price: a man's health. A study by the University of Canberra, Australia, in 2011 shows that people who are unhappy at work suffer from depression, anxiety, and stress, sometimes even the same as or worse than those who don't have a job at all; and when one is dissatisfied with work, the decision to change jobs comes easily. Sinek points the blame less at the nature of the job and more towards weak management and leadership, as the absence of a sense of belongingness breeds disloyalty.

Similarly, according to a study by the University College, London, people who don't feel recognized enough for their efforts at work tend to suffer from heart disease. The results of a Gallup poll in 2013 also shows that when leaders ignore their employees, 40 percent of them become detached from their work; and surprisingly, only 22 percent do the same when criticized by the boss. This shows that it's the acknowledgment itself that matters. And when receiving positive recognition, only one percent of employees disengage from the job. Sinek emphasizes that it's the companies that nurture misery that reach their demise.

The Whitehall Studies

The Whitehall Studies were conducted by scientists in Britain to examine the correlation between an individual's rank on the corporate ladder and stress. The researchers discovered that stress wasn't caused by higher ranking but by a lower degree of control that an employee feels throughout the workday. Surprising results were also found in a 2012 study by Harvard and Stanford on Harvard's executive MBA program, showing that leaders had lower stress levels than their subordinates.

Results from the Whitehall Studies dramatically show that stress-induced health risks and mental illness are more present in those with lower ranks and not the other way around as commonly believed. But Sinek emphasizes that going up the hierarchy is not the solution. Rather, it is an empowering, safe, and supportive work environment that can improve workers' lives. Despite all this data, people have settled for uncomfortable work environments and do nothing to improve them. The solution is not necessarily to leave but to adopt a new attitude by focusing on others in the workplace rather than ourselves, believing that, like the Spartans, one's strength comes from each other's protection.

A study from Boston College shows that children are affected not by how long their parents are out for work, but by the mood they bring home afterwards. So even if one believes that putting up with the misery at work is the responsible way of helping the home, in truth, it's doing the family more harm. The leaders of companies must build and maintain Circles of Safety in the workplace in order to eliminate the risks to the health and welfare of employees.

Powerful Forces

When Enough Was Enough

Sinek paints a picture of human life in the Paleolithic era to emphasize how human physiology and cooperative instincts have allowed man to survive a world void of modern advantages. Back then, there was no question of whether or not man needed to cooperate with one another; humans automatically recognized this essentiality and successfully faced danger together. Today's leaders need to understand that this primal instinct remains true; that if members of an organization are preoccupied with protecting themselves from one another, both outside threats and opportunities will be missed.

In the Beginning...

Because of cooperation, man not only survived but also thrived. Our capability of working together enabled us to change the environment to suit our needs rather than changing ourselves to suit our conditions. Our genetic coding is unchanged, but our world has modernized, and this comes with both advantages and costs.

It's All About the Group

Back when we were simple hunters and gatherers, humans gave the utmost importance to trust and cooperative relationships. Protecting our own was top priority, especially when there were more than enough dangers from the external forces of nature. This was true across all continents of the world, proving that it wasn't the environment that prompted the behavior but the human design itself. Social interactions and bonds had been as essential to organizations then as they are now.

Our Chemical Dependency

Aside from the survival instinct hardwired into man's physiology, the quest for happiness is also deeply ingrained within us. There exists an incentive system that conditions us to behave in certain ways in exchange for rewards: positive feelings caused by chemicals in the human body. For happiness, they are endorphins, dopamine, serotonin, and oxytocin.

The Paradox of Being Human

Although it is essential to behave with the collective in consideration, humans can't help but weigh concern for themselves versus the tribe. This creates conflict of interest, also present in our genetic code. The first two "happy" chemicals in human biology, endorphins and dopamine, are coined by Sinek as "selfish" chemicals because their purpose is to drive an individual to care for himself: finding food, building shelter, inventing tools. In contrast, the "selfless" chemicals, serotonin and oxytocin, encourage us to work together by making us feel trustful and loyal. Finding the right balance between self-interest and that of the community is the key to our long-term survival.

E.D.S.O.

Without Selfish Chemicals, We Would Starve to Death

Though it seems logical for us to go hunting only when we feel hungry, it's highly inconvenient in the practical sense. Today, we find ourselves shopping for groceries even when we're not experiencing hunger pangs. The selfish chemicals, endorphins and dopamine, drive us to hunt and gather, enabling our survival and progress.

E Is for Endorphins

The endorphin chemical acts like an opiate, giving us pleasure instead of stress and discomfort, an experience of the "runner's high." This biological response gave us an advantage in the Paleolithic era when it was necessary to travel great distances while hunting. Another behavior that helps the body release endorphins is laughter. A little lightheartedness can go a long way in reducing tension and preventing us from being afraid.

D Is for Dopamine: An Incentive for Progress

Dopamine makes us feel satisfaction after accomplishing a task. In terms of hunting and gathering, dopamine provides us the good feeling from eating a meal, encouraging us to repeat this behavior. Increasing progress also increases dopamine levels in the body, andin the moment we achieve our goal, we get the biggest hit of the dopamine chemical as a reward, making us biased towards progress.

Generosity and Other Ways to Build Trust

Whenever we receive and provide help, the body gives us small shots of oxytocin. Even those who simply witness the act get their dose, too. This is the scientific basis of "paying it forward." Physical contact also triggers the reaction. Athletes high-five each other, children cling to their parents, and world leaders shake hands upon confirming a mutual agreement.

The Big C

Another benefit of living in groups is that each member can protect the tribe by watching out for danger. We have a biological early warning system built into our body that helps us sense imminent threats. Johnny Bravo's encounter in Afghanistan is the perfect example. He and his twenty-two men all had that "gut feeling" that something was wrong. This feeling is caused by the chemical cortisol. Such scenarios aren't limited to life-threatening experiences like combat or predation. For instance, forthcoming layoffs in an office scenario is a form of pressing danger. And when the actual threat presents itself, we get a large dose of adrenaline that boosts our strength to fight for ourselves. Otherwise, we wait for the cortisol to leave our bloodstream as we return to a relaxed state.

The fact is that cortisol wasn't intended for long-term presence within our bodies, as the stress it causes is serious. In a less-than-ideal environment, the existence of a constant low-grade anxiety inhibits the formation of a Circle of Safety, thereby threatening the survival of all members of the group. There is no trust or bond between workers and leaders, signs of impending danger are kept secret for the purposes of self-preservation; and the cortisol keeps coursing through the veins, inhibiting the release of oxytocin. This starts a counterproductive cycle. In time, we learn to cope with this unhealthy condition, unaware of the slow destruction it inflicts upon the mind and body: in the face of immediate danger, cortisol tags the immune system as a nonessential element for responding to the threat. Thus, the constant presence of cortisol makes us vulnerable to sickness. It is then no surprise that the demands of the modern world have coincided with an increase in cases of cancer, heart disease and the like. A good

How We Got Here

The Boom Before the Bust

It was after World War I, the Roaring Twenties, when America experienced a commercial and consumerist boom. The people had money, and advancements in technology and media made waves all throughout the country. New industries sprang forth, creating new demands, but with all the excess came a lot of waste as well. The Depression was the inevitable result, but in 1941 the attack on Pearl Harbor forced America out of the slump and into World War II. It was during this time that the entire country, the Greatest Generation, worked together for a cause. And so as the country left the time of war and welcomed the 1950s, a sense of hard work, cooperation, and loyalty had been instilled into the consciousness of the people. All seemed well, but not for long.

The Eight-Hundred-Pound Boomer in the Room

After the war came the sudden growth in population: the Baby Boom, adding 76 million Americans to the citizenry from the 1950s to 1964. Unlike their parents, the Greatest Generation, the Boomers had grown up in wealth and prosperity, and the differences between the two generations created tension. The maturing Boomers grew up to be more selfish and concerned only for their own happiness: the "Me" decade, as Thomas Wolfe describes in a 1976 *New York* magazine. Modern theories about conducting business became known in the late 1970s, and people were inclined to focus on protecting personal wealth. By the time the 1980s and 1990s rolled in, the Boomer generation had risen to positions of power, forever changing the face of the nation.

The Boomers All Grown Up

In the 1980s, Bill Gates had been the young founder of Microsoft, envisioning "a PC on every desk." The development of computers and other technology encouraged individualism and ease of use through disposability, even in the aspect of people as expendable resources.

The Day We Embraced Layoffs

On August 5, 1981, President Ronald Reagan fired 11,359 air traffic controllers who were members of the PATCO union. They were demanding higher pay and lesser work hours, but negotiation talks had been unsuccessful. On August 3, they went on strike, provoking Reagan to ban every last one of them from working for the FAA. It isn't a question of whether or not Reagan's actions were justified. Rather, it's a matter of what message he sent to the leaders of the business world. He may not have intended it, but this event introduced the idea of saving the organization from economic failure at the expense of the people's protection as the sensible first choice rather than the last resort. This is in total contrast to the protection that our anthropological nature expects from our leaders. We forget that in the first place, it is the people who are the most valuable resources of the organization as they are the inventors and innovators of the products and services that bring success. Nonetheless, many company leaders have succumbed to the expectations of outside entities, unknowingly reducing their own company's capacity to perform.

When Leaders Eat First

The stock market crashes resulting from the unintentional mismanagement of resources by the Boomers indicate how the modern environments we've created for ourselves have frustrated our natural inclinations for trust and cooperation towards survival. The business society has implemented a set of norms that are more dopamine-driven (short-term achievement) and less serotonin- and oxytocin-driven (long-term community progress). This imbalance caused the stock market crash, an event that displays the natural tendency of the world to correct itself and regain balance, a phenomenon that has resounded throughout our history. Today, we lack true leaders who abide by empathy and humanity; and so the vicious cycle goes on.

Dehumanization

Amidst the abundance of the modern world, our anthropological assessment of the value of things is abstracted: the more we have of a certain thing, the less we value it – until the essential human concepts lose their meaning. The idea of a person is diminished when he is viewed as nothing but a consumer, an online profile, employee, or expense. We struggle to cooperate in a world of strangers. We must find a way to eliminate the abstraction that can damage our economy.

The Abstract Challenge

Abstraction Kills

The aftermath of the Nazi genocide of World War II posed the question of what had driven such a massive number of people to commit crimes against humanity, and the simplest answer was that they were "just following orders." In 1961, Stanley Milgram, a psychologist from Yale, studied the extent of human obedience to authority. He experimented on 160 volunteers, the "teachers," commanding them to flip a series of switches specifically labeled to give the impression that they were activating varying degrees of electric shock affecting another person, the "student." In truth, the student was also a researcher pretending to feel pain from the shocks he received. When the teachers could hear the student's reactions to the "pain," a majority strongly opposed continuing the experiment. But when the student had been placed in a different room, unheard except for thumping on the walls, a majority of the teachers proceeded to flip the switches all the way to the highest degree of shock; all because the scientist, the higher authority, told them to continue.

When the truth was revealed, some participants still felt remorse for their actions while others ended up blaming the scientist and even the student, stating that he was "stupid" and "deserved to be shocked." The takeaway is that in the duration of the experiment, no one asked about the well-being of the student in the other room. They were more concerned about saving their own skins from the consequences of disobedience. Although Milgram's experiment is obviously unethical, it proves to show the scale with which abstraction can allow us to become inhuman.

Modern Abstraction

Milgram's Findings Come to Life

When the impact of our words and actions are abstracted from our view, we are taken down the dangerous path of harming other people for self-preservation. In modern society, for example, we can find concrete cases of food industry companies who value money over people so much that they are prepared to sell corrupted products to increase profit, risking the health of the public. When we detach ourselves from the people we hurt, it's easier for us to focus on our selfish desires and find any justifications for our actions, valid or not.

The Responsibility of Business

Capitalist entities justify their actions by referencing the letter of the law as long as they can use its loopholes for personal gain, even when it allows them to turn a blind eye from moral responsibility. For instance, Apple, Inc. does not deny its taking advantage of weaknesses in the tax laws that allowed it to keep $74 billion from the IRS. Technically, they broke no rules. But the human sense of right and wrong is seen from beyond the perspective of the law.

Within the Law

Like Apple, the Oceanic Steam Navigation Company, owner of the *Titanic*, evaded additional costs by simply following the rules: they carried only sixteen inflatable rafts as required by law even when it needed four times that number to fit all passengers. Thus, more than half of the passengers died when the ship sank.

We need leaders who can provide us with a higher and noble authority, a moral code, to empower us to do the right thing even when we have to sacrifice our self-interests. Like Johnny Bravo who, instead of staying safe above the clouds, chose to risk his life for his men, we are still capable of managing abstraction.

Managing the Abstraction

Numbers of People Aren't People, They're Numbers

When we use numbers to represent people, we agree with Stalin who famously said that "the death of one man is a tragedy" but "the death of a million is a statistic." Human life loses meaning when we see numbers rather than the people in need of aid. Empathy falters. Our innovations only ever mean anything when they recognize the real people behind the numbers.

Rule 1. Keep It Real – Bring People Together

The internet has made the problem of abstraction even more complex. It provides the screen behind which people can hide after displaying distasteful behavior.

Online relationships seem real to us, but they are only truly legitimized when we meet face-to-face. Real trust can only be built through live interaction; virtual trust doesn't exist.

Rule 2. Keep It Manageable – Obey Dunbar's Number

Robin Dunbar, a British anthropologist and professor at Oxford University, concluded that a person cannot maintain more than 150 close relationships. The earliest groups of *Homo sapiens* and even a company of Marines are each composed of only about 150 people. Any more and the system will most likely collapse. This is why senior leaders designate midlevel leaders to manage larger groups. Dunbar's research proves that when a group gets bigger than 150 members, levels of cooperation and hard work decline. Our anthropological design dictates that we only really care for people we personally know, and the larger the group, the fewer chances we have of forming trusting relationships with everyone.

Rule 3. Meet the People You Help

It is imperative for humans to see tangible proof of our work's meaning in order to feel motivated to do better. For instance, a bank's employees would gain inspiration from people who testify about how their bank loans have saved their homes and families. Unfortunately, most organizations of today are lacking in this aspect, relying on figures to display the results of human efforts. Being social animals, humans would respond better not with unfeeling numbers but with a humane sense of purpose.

Rule 4. Give Them Time, Not Just Money

Our tribal inclinations have taught us to value time and effort spent for us above everything else. But in modern society, money has become the concrete representation of effort, though not quite as valuable as the real thing. A person's time and energy are finite, while money can be earned and accumulated. Thus, an organization can't buy the loyalty of its members with money alone. We get a dose of feel-good chemicals when we give and receive money, but it doesn't last long, and it doesn't create an impact on others the same way time and effort could. For example, a notorious CEO won't be able to restore a good reputation just by donating to charity. Giving and receiving time and effort runs both ways for leaders and their people.

Rule 5. Be Patient – The Rule of Seven Days and Seven Years

It should take more than seven days and fewer than seven years before we can correctly decide whether or not our relationship with a person is truly a bond of human trust. Our modern world is filled with instant gratification: short-term shots of dopamine. We get what we want, and we get it now. It's convenient when we're researching online or shopping, but we mustn't forget that forming true relationships takes patience.

Imbalance

In ancient times, humans never had more than they needed. Some had more surplus than others, and any mismanagement tends to create imbalance leading to "destructive abundance." Integrity falters and the absence of cooperation breeds unhealthy politics. This is a result wherein the members of an organization give more value to results than people and purpose.

Destructive Abundance

Leadership Lesson 1: So Goes the Culture, So Goes the Company

A Culture Sacrificed

From the 1970s to the 1990s, Goldman Sachs was a firm that operated under the ideal of "long-term greed." This meant that its members were willing to take hits if it would ensure the loyalty of their clients and help them reap benefits in the long run. But well into the 1990s, a new dopamine-driven culture had been introduced, and the organization was split between the old Goldman built on loyalty and the new Goldman built on numbers and short-term goals. By 2010, Goldman Sachs had become a symbol of excess and greed, a sign of their watered-down culture. Internally, teams were pitted against one another, and nobody felt safe about their job. Employment at Goldman used to mean being "boy scouts," something more than an occupation. But none of its workers identify with the company as proudly as before because the culture of an organization reflects on the character of its people. Things could've ended differently if the organization's leaders hadn't allowed the destructive culture to take hold.

Bad Cultures Breed Bad Leaders

Kim Stewart described the culture at Citigroup to be that of self-preservation and fear. A crab mentality had permeated the system, and employees withheld information from one another in order to get the advantage. Inevitably, the company suffered financial losses and mass layoffs. But the leadership hadn't been humbled by its defeat. Stewart's boss still managed to say he wasn't going to be the mentor who could give her career advice. So goes the culture.

A Culture Protected

When Spencer Silver, a scientist at 3M, failed to develop a strong adhesive, he wasn't afraid to share his failure with his colleagues as he thought the others may find a way to improve it. This was how Post-it Notes were invented. The company's innovation was so strong that even in the tough economy of 2009, 3M managed to launch more than a thousand new products. Their culture is a Circle of Safety wherein people trust one another enough to share both successes and failures. Their culture of cooperation and sharing paved the way for innovation.

Leadership Lesson 2: So Goes the Leader, so Goes the Culture

I Before You. Me Before We.

Many modern organizations consider an employee-centric culture to be weak. This gives birth to dictatorships – not just in governments but also in the workspace where the leaders are unfeeling, absolute authorities ready to expend the people for profit, self-interest, and control. This was the case with Stanley O'Neal at Merrill Lynch in 2001, who had alienated himself from his employees and encouraged internal competition. By October 2007, the company lost billions of dollars, and O'Neal's reign had come to an end – there was nobody left in the organization willing to support him.

In the *Atlantic Monthly*, Mark Bowden wrote, "Power gradually shuts the tyrant off from the world." A leader who works purely for self-interest creates a cortisol-driven culture that will lead to nothing but collapse.

True Power

When Captain Marquet was transferred to the USS *Santa Fe*, he had been used to having full control of his ship. When he issued orders, the crew followed him blindly. Until one day he ordered his navigator to turn up the speed to two-thirds setting. The submarine didn't go any faster. Captain Marquet didn't know that the *Santa Fe* was unlike the ship he was trained for, the *Olympia*; and so there was no two-thirds setting. He asked the navigator, who knew all along, why he had relayed the order despite the fact. The officer only responded with, "Because you told me to."

Captain Marquet realized that those on top had all the authority, but those at the bottom had all the information. In any organization, being trained solely for compliance isn't enough. The leader shouldn't be the only one made accountable for the success and failure of the group. Rather, he is responsible for ensuring the success and protection of each member of his crew. The captain changed the culture of his team from permission to intent, literally banning the words "permission to" aboard the ship and replacing it with "I intend." This culture had improved the crew's performance so much that, from being the lowest rated U.S. submarine fleet, the *Santa Fe* had become the best-rated crew in Navy history.

Physics defines power as the transfer of energy. Organizations work the same way – the more energy is distributed across the system, the more each part of the body functions and empowers the leader.

Leadership Lesson 3: Integrity Matters

The Foxhole Test

The Circle of Safety in the Marine Corps is built on trust and integrity. The absence of these two qualities can mean certain death. No one in the group is expected to be right all the time, but each member must be prepared to take responsibility for his actions. True leadership isn't saying what we want to hear but what we *need* to hear. The same applies to every other organization, even when the situations within aren't matters of life and death.

How Not to Build Trust

Trust isn't awarded instantaneously. We constantly assess the information that people give us, and if their words and actions are consistent with their intentions, we see integrity in them. Thus, integrity is not a state of mind but rather a practice that is exhibited when we are ready to be honest with each other even in the face of disagreement or mistakes. Any attempts to protect one's image at all costs is considered suspicious. For example, we know that politicians who seem too agreeable during campaign season may be adopting a superficial façade, while those who show their less perfect, human side are deemed trustworthy in their authenticity. This is particularly important for leaders since their subordinates would almost always follow them blindly, believing they only have the best intentions for the group void of self-interest and abstraction. If this is the culture adopted by a leader, his members would do the same. But if they fail to tell the truth, the bond of trust is broken. Ultimately, the question we must ask ourselves is, "Would I want to be in the same foxhole as my leader?"

A Corporate Lesson in Telling the Truth

No company can guarantee that all their actions would be 100% fail-safe; everyone understands that. The important thing is to be honest about one's mistakes. The Bank of America, for example, received a lot of backlash for wanting to charge their clients an additional five dollars per month for making purchases using their debit card. They were forced to retract the decision after so much public outrage, but in doing so they weren't honest about the necessity of charging the fee and why they changed their mind. If they had been straightforward about it, the situation would've turned in their favor, and their reputation could've been enhanced by their honesty. But they weren't ready to admit vulnerability. Hence, the people didn't trust the Bank of America enough to be in the same foxhole with them.

Leadership Lesson 4: Friends Matter

To Win or to Serve

From the 1960s to 1980s, politics in Washington functioned relatively well despite its members belonging to opposing parties. The measure of success wasn't based on who held the majority but rather on who got the work done. But in the early 1990s, Newt Gingrich, a Republican, determined it was necessary for his party to hold the majority, leaving cooperation out of the picture. The two parties were distanced from one another; there was little opportunity to build relationships based on trust. It had become all about serving one's own district rather than the collective as politicians spent more time fundraising and building personal power. Hostilities between parties were at their peak, and Congress had become an ineffective governing body. It has gone as far as the public blaming the Congress' lack of collaboration for the economic crisis of 2008.

Enemies Fight. Friends Cooperate.

The friendship between Bob Goodlatte, a Republican congressman from Virginia and Stephanie Herseth

Sandlin, a Democratic congresswoman from South Dakota proves that, despite being adversaries at work, it's possible to set aside differences and build a bond of trust. They paid attention to each other, and when they disagreed, they compromised, simply because they knew cooperation doesn't have to mean unquestioned agreement. Rather, it's working together for the greater good. Their friendship has become a model for others in government.

Leadership Lesson 5: Lead the People, Not the Numbers

Neutron Jack

In the 1970s, we learned how in reality a company's share price alone wasn't an indicator of its success. In response, corporate America assumed a movement that gave primary focus to shareholder value as the main fuel of the economy. Business pioneers took companies with undervalued stocks, cut expenses, and focused on maximizing shareholder value. In the 1980s, Jack Welch, CEO of General Electric, adopted this principle, laying off the bottom 10 percent of his managers while rewarding the top 20 percent with stocks. This "rank and yank" strategy earned him the nickname "Neutron

Jack." Under his leadership, GE had become the most valuable company in the world.

But this system was only beneficial for the short-term. When Welch left, he took his expertise with him. We must remember that a true leader creates a long-lasting legacy and distributes power amongst the organization's people by building and protecting them. Unfortunately, using layoffs to meet target numbers had become the trend. Leaders have overlooked the fact that people are not expendable resources. By the 1990s, the culture of empathy within corporations was not to be seen. Stock manipulation and financial fraud increased. Luckily, in more recent years, modern thinkers have enlightened us about how employee value is greater than shareholder value.

Boom and Bust

Eventually, Welch himself had expressed his realization that focusing on shareholder value had been the "dumbest idea in the world." Many big companies have taken a deep dive by cutting corners to meet short-term goals, creating much more damage to themselves and to other entities in the long run. Welch responded by saying that a company's main constituencies are employees, customers, and products.

Leadership by the People

James Sinegal, co-founder of Costco, conducted business in a way that is completely opposite to Welch. Sinegal hadn't been a household name, but for good reason: he let his people take the credit. The balanced culture he promoted is the main reason his company has thrived throughout the years. His support for a culture of empathy, a strong Circle of Safety, has enabled him to ensure the survival of his company long after he's gone. In the recession of 2008, Costco still gained annual profits of over $1 billion even when they had been paying the highest wages in the retail business. All leaders must follow his example and remember that customers won't love a company until its employees love it first.

A Society of Addicts

At the Center of All Our Problems Is Us

Enlightenment

Before the Age of Reason, people didn't want to believe that the negligence of doctors could spread disease. During the 18th and 19th centuries' puerperal fever epidemic in Europe and America, doctors weren't required to sterilize their tools or wash their hands during treatment, indirectly causing the further spread of the sickness. Those who had been enlightened enough to criticize this were shot down until twelve years later when the medical community admitted responsibility. The same idea applies to leaders: whenever they are the cause of the problem, they have to be ready to admit it.

A Very Modern Addiction

The availability of addictive substances like alcohol, nicotine, and drugs has given humans a shortcut to the dopamine high. The human body wasn't built for these conditions, and so the chemical that was designed to help us survive is now rewarding us for destructive behavior. It is the same with today's corporate cultures: incentive systems have created a dopamine-driven addiction to performance.

Have a Dopamine Addiction. You Earned It!

Like our prehistoric ancestors in a successful hunt, the modern business world gives us dopamine shots with each target hit. But the unbalanced culture dominated by short-term goals and personal incentives has discouraged collaboration, hindering the development of a Circle of Safety. Like all addictions, this dopamine-driven system has consequences: a total disregard for others in the name of self-interest.

At Any Expense

The quality of the news business has declined further and further as what used to be an unbiased public service has become a capitalist enterprise. In response, media regulations were implemented to make sure that the news industry doesn't become profit-driven. Yet the news has ended up feeding the consumerist mind with overblown entertainment rather than socially relevant facts. The problem comes from media executives who are driven by ratings and not purpose. If only these execs would set aside the drive to win and give way to service for the people, the news business would become a healthy organization once more.

More! More! More!

The dopamine-driven Boomer generation had created systems within the banking industry that broke the law to serve self-interest, and any attempts to fix the corrupt system were repealed. This created the numerous economic crashes of the past decades. Sinek recognizes the impending threat to the entire nation's Circle of Safety as one "addicted" generation is replaced by another.

The Abstract Generation

The Biggest Losers

The Greatest Generation raised their children, the Boomers, to the life of plenty that they never got to enjoy. In turn, the Boomers raised their children to be wary of those who stand in the way of what they want. And so Generations X and Y have developed a sense of entitlement – a form of impatience driven by the misconception that success and happiness come instantly. They grew up in an economy that puts numbers first before people: a culture of abstraction that could make them the biggest losers courtesy of their parents' excess.

The Distracted Generation

Growing up surrounded by many technologies, Generation Y assumed that it was great with multitasking. In truth, it is merely being distracted. The proof is out there: between 2000 and 2010, cases of attention deficit hyperactivity disorder (ADHD) have spiked. Children are now developing an addiction to distraction caused by activities like text messaging and online correspondence. If the phone rings while we're driving, we feel the necessity to look despite the safety risk. Gen Y is getting its dopamine high from things that satisfy "faster" and "now." Commitment becomes harder, and addressing the problems of society come in the form of "raising awareness" rather than remedies. The youth is driven by dopamine shots from campaigning for causes rather than serotonin and oxytocin rewards from actually helping others. This allows antisocial behavior to fester.

The Dire Scenario

Disillusioned, the younger generations have become more inclined to depression, suicide, and the antisocial mindset. Sinek predicts that it will only get worse with future generations because they will have grown up relying on prescription drugs and online support groups rather than biological bonds of friendship and love. Our primitive mammal brain leads us to conclude that without a sense of belongingness we must be abandoned and left for dead. The good news is that we hold the solution ourselves.

Becoming A Leader

Step 12

We are the architects of our own demise. The first step to recovery from our modern addiction, like in Alcoholics Anonymous, is to admit that we are addicted. In AA, those who find sobriety are the ones that complete Step Twelve: the commitment to help another person fight the addiction. AA meetings are conducted in recreational centers and basements rather than online chat rooms for a reason: real connections where people feel safe are required to beat the condition. These bonds last well after the program. AA is a perfectly built Circle of Safety.

In Oxytocin We Trust

The presence of serotonin in our biological design is for the purpose of reinforcing relationships. It works best with the feelings of trust and love that are made possible by oxytocin. This chemical has functioned towards prevention rather than cure: there is evidence that high levels of oxytocin gained from acts of selflessness actually prevent addiction in the first place. It suppresses cortisol, helps us live longer and it solidifies the Circle of Safety wherein we draw strength from honest human bonds void of self-preservation. Through this, difficulties seem easier to endure.

Shared Struggle

Want Not, Waste Anyway

Fifty percent of our food resources are discarded as waste. This is the consequence of having much more than what is essential for survival. Our biggest challenge now is to collectively feel the burden of commoditization and pull together to eradicate it. What used to be marvels of innovation have lost their value due to abundance, especially when we don't have to work for them anymore.

Our Best Days at Work

The fondest memories we have from work are usually those where hardships were shared. We recall with affection not the struggle but the camaraderie that, through the feel-good reward given by oxytocin, helps us grow closer biologically. Thus, we must redefine the hardship of this modern age of abundance – not by living in extreme austerity but by confining our futures according to our means.

Redefining the Struggle

Our abundant society has become stagnant like a large, successful corporation. We are no longer as driven to survive because we have everything we need and more. Thus, we must frame our goals according to our size. For instance, Bill Gates aims for Microsoft to put a PC on every desk. Despite the company's massive achievements, this goal is a long way from being accomplished, thereby inspiring further innovation. If all leaders do the same and give their people a challenge that towers over their resources but not their abilities, the people would do everything to overcome it.

The Value of Purpose

Stanley Milgram's experiment on human obedience and authority demonstrated how belief in a higher power than the scientist gave the subjects strength against following orders blindly. In the case of society, the drive to serve oneself ranks lower than service to others. We draw more inspiration from causes bigger than ourselves. In the end, we need leaders who can give us the ultimate cause that will encourage commitment to one another.

We Need More Leaders

Johnny Bravo explains that empathy is a service that a leader owes to everyone. Sadly, many of today's leaders follow Jack Welch's approach, so much so that the entire economy is unbalanced. Although the movement we want to push for is huge, this change can only happen gradually. We must start to do small acts of goodness towards others one day at a time and in doing so, become the leaders ourselves.

Acknowledgements

Sinek thanked all those who supported him while completing his book, as well as the readers of his so-called "ramblings." His publisher, research assistant, and other colleagues who kept him on track were among the people he specifically mentioned. He also gave appreciation to those in various branches of the military for taking care of him during trips and for sharing their remarkable stories.

Conclusion

There is one resounding challenge presented to us in this book: step up and become leaders ourselves so that our global community can have a culture of empathy and eradicate the culture of selfishness that threatens to kill us. This is the only way that mankind can develop a worldwide Circle of Safety that will protect it from self-destruction. Simon Sinek shows us that this goal is possible, providing concrete examples of admirable men and women who have answered this call-to-action, giving emphasis on the strong foundations found within successful companies and in the military. Johnny Bravo shared with his team an incorruptible bond because he was void of self-interest: a true leader. He put his people first. He treated his men like family. And because of the healthy culture he promoted, they escaped enemy fire and survived – a reflection of how all other organizations may overcome external dangers and threats to survival.

We overlook the fact that the answer to sustaining human organizations has actually been in our hands all this time. The biggest problem of today is that humanity has managed to view people as nothing but variables towards selfish gain and personal accomplishments. It may seem like a complex, modern issue with a complex, modern solution; but the truth is we can reference the efficacy of our primitive tribal systems to address this. Sinek reminds us of how Paleolithic man valued cooperation and trust within their communities, allowing mankind to become a successful species. They didn't study anthropological theories, business plans, or combat strategies to defeat the external forces that threatened them. They relied on naturally occurring chemicals in human physiology: endorphins, dopamine, serotonin, and oxytocin, all of which create an incentive system that encourages essential human behaviors. They make us feel good whenever we commit acts that benefit not only ourselves but the rest of the tribe, and they suppress any negative feelings that may discourage us from performing our responsibilities to the group. A natural balance between these chemicals must be achieved, and a leader must oversee this balance by setting the organization on the right course.

Summary of Lean In

By: Sheryl Sandberg

Proudly Brought to you by:

Text Copyright © Readtrepreneur

Legal & Disclaimer

resulting from the application of any of the information provided by this guide. This disclaimer applies to any damages or injury caused by the use and application, whether directly or indirectly, of any advice or information presented, whether for breach of contract, tort, negligence, personal injury, criminal intent, or under any other cause of action.

You agree to accept all risks of using the information presented inside this book. You need to consult a professional medical practitioner in order to ensure you are both able and healthy enough to participate in this program.

Table of Contents

The Book at a Glance

For a long time, many people didn't realize that women were quietly suffering, not seeking any special attention whenever they experienced hardships in life. The good news is that today, people are starting to put more effort into creating ways to empower women.

Women before us struggled to defend the rights that women now assume. Some women even feel highly appreciative when they try to compare the life they have with other women from all over the world. Many countries still deny the basic rights of women. Still, even if situations can get worse, we should always strive to make things better. We can try to turn the vision into reality, where men and women are equal.

Unfortunately, men still rule the world. There are only a few countries governed by women. Although women are continuously surpassing men in terms of educational achievements, the progression towards the top of industries has ceased. This means the voices of women are not equally heard when making decisions that influence the world.

In the workforce, things remain the same. We must face the

obstruction of our revolution. If we truly want an equal world, women should be running half the countries and men should be running half the homes. This way, the world will surely become a better place for all.

More women should aspire to leadership roles where they can strongly voice their needs or concerns. This can be a good step towards improving their conditions. But first, we must think of ways to remove the barriers that prevent women from reaching the top.

Women are confronted by real obstacles in terms of their professional life. They have a constant need to prove and validate themselves, far more than men. In fact, it has been reported that when it comes to promotion, people see men's potential while they only see women's past accomplishments.

The hurdles that live within them also restrain women. They hold themselves back in various ways. They lack self-confidence, and they seldom raise their hands. Instead of leaning in, they are always pulling themselves back. They believe it when society tells them it's wrong for women to be aggressive, outspoken, or more influential than men. Because of this, they have lower expectations when it comes to their own achievements.

To gain power, women need to know that it is possible to

eliminate these internal hurdles. This book identifies several complex challenges that they face and centers on the changes and differences that can be made. This doesn't offer perfect solutions, but it stems from data, research, observations, learning, and experiences.

This book is for every woman at any stage of her life and career who aims to make it to the top or simply go after her goals. Likewise, this is for every man who wishes to further understand the struggles that women face so he can help create a truly equal world.

This doesn't mean that everyone should have similar objectives. Some people get satisfaction from living life just the way they want to. Each of us has our own specific path, and we determine which goals suit our lives, dreams, and values.

Hopefully, this book inspires not just women but also men. This is a conversation that cannot be ignored. We need to keep fighting for every right we have, especially women's rights. It's how we can move one step closer towards true equality.

FREE BONUSES

P.S. Is it okay if we overdeliver?

Here at Readtrepreneur Publishing, we believe in overdelivering way beyond our reader's expectations. Is it okay if we overdeliver?

Here's the deal, we're going to give you an extremely condensed PDF summary of the book which you've just read and much more…

What's the catch? We need to trust you… You see, we want to overdeliver and in order for us to do that, we've to trust our reader to keep this bonus a secret to themselves? Why? Because we don't want people to be getting our exclusive PDF summaries even without buying our books itself. Unethical, right?

Ok. Are you ready?

Firstly, remember that your book is code: "**READ50**".

Next, visit this link: **http://bit.ly/exclusivepdfs**

Everything else will be self explanatory after you've visited: **http://bit.ly/exclusivepdfs.**

We hope you'll enjoy our free bonuses as much as we enjoyed preparing it for you!

1: The Leadership Ambition

What Would You Do if You Weren't Afraid?

Sheryl's grandmother, Rosalind Einhorn, came from a poor family living in a tiny, crowded apartment near their relatives. Those relatives called the boys by their real names, while the girls were only addressed as "Girlie."

At the time of the Depression, Rosalind left high school so she could assist in their household, helping her mother resell undergarments for a small profit. During that time, boys weren't pulled from school because their education was considered the hope of their family so they could climb the social and financial ladder. Meanwhile, girls' education was of little importance. They were only expected to manage a decent home. Fortunately, Rosalind was given the chance to go back to school. She even graduated from U.C. Berkeley.

After college, she worked selling accessories and pocketbooks at David's Fifth Avenue. When she left her job for marriage, family legend claimed the business owner needed four people to take her place. Years later she displayed her wisdom regarding business to help save her family from bankruptcy.

She emphasized education for all her children. Sheryl's

mother attended the co-ed University of Pennsylvania where she studied French literature. After graduating, she studied the American workforce and came to believe that women only had two options in terms of career, either nursing or teaching. Her mother chose to teach. When she became pregnant with Sheryl, she dropped out of her Ph.D. program. Back then, husbands were thought weak if their wives helped them support their families.

Although Sheryl was raised in a conventional home, she and her siblings were taught how important it was to do great in school and do equal chores, as well as to participate in extracurricular activities. Although Sheryl wasn't particularly athletic growing up, she was raised to believe that girls can do anything the boys can do. She was welcome to choose any career path there was.

In college, all of her classmates paid equal attention to academics. Males and females challenged one another in activities, classes, and even job interviews. It seemed the playing field had been leveled. Yet twenty years later, the world hadn't changed all that much. Her male classmates had gotten jobs in a professional environment, while her female counterparts either worked outside the home or became full-time mothers staying at home. Women who are highly trained are leaving the workforce. As a result, organizations invest much more in men since they seem more likely to stay longer in the workforce.

Many women strove to give more women choices; however, it didn't cross their minds that many would simply choose to drop out of the workforce. Combining personal and professional goals appeared to be more difficult than they had expected. The workplace wasn't able to provide the flexibility that women need to fulfill their responsibilities at home.

Women, without a doubt, possess the skills needed to lead in the workplace. Even though they are already surpassing men when it comes to academic achievements, they still remain unacknowledged inside the workplace. They are discouraged from taking risks or promoting themselves.

Many women are professionally driven, just like men, but more men aim for the superior jobs. Compared to women, men find it more appealing to have powerful, challenging jobs with more responsibilities. They consider it a priority to strive for a managerial position. Nevertheless, change is beginning to happen since more women are finding it important to be successful in their high-paying career. Still, there remains a gap in leadership ambition because millennial women don't really see themselves as visionaries or leaders.

Also, in our culture, being remarkably ambitious isn't entirely a compliment for women.

On top of a woman's career, marriage continues to be emphasized. Society stresses that it would be less likely for women to find suitable men if they go after their career. However, ambition isn't really the problem. It's just that women are more knowledgeable about various and more significant goals. There are numerous ways to have a great impact, not just aspiring for leadership roles. Still, societal expectations inform the way people consider their accomplishments.

Girls receive messages that clearly discourage leadership rather than praise their motivating outer traits. For instance, a girl trying to lead is called bossy. But it's unlikely for boys to be tagged as bossy since being a boss is neither offensive nor surprising.

Society encourages boys to give their opinions even at an early age, while girls are reminded to raise their hands before speaking. It still prevails among grownups. Authority figures continue to silence female voices. Because society defines what the appropriate behavior is for women, they end up silencing themselves.

All through our lives, the gender stereotypes instilled during childhood are strengthened. Leadership roles are mostly filled by men, which is why women don't look forward to attaining them. People believe women earn less because men usually earn more.

The basic impression for men is that they can have both a satisfying personal life and a flourishing professional life. Meanwhile, the impression for women is that it's difficult and even impossible to have both. It's a great thing that today, women no longer need to worry about having both their families and careers. They can become successful no matter what they choose to do, whether it's having professional or personal fulfillment or even both.

2: Sit at the Table

A couple of years back, Sheryl arranged a meeting, inviting several executives for a discussion concerning the economy. She turned to the women and encouraged them to sit at the table alongside the men, but they refused and remained seated at the side of the room.

When the meeting was over, Sheryl explained to the women that they should've joined the others at the table since they were publicly welcomed. The women seemed surprised at first, but they agreed afterward. It was a moment where Sheryl witnessed how women's internal hurdles can change their behavior. Aside from dealing with organizational issues, women are also fighting a battle that's deep within them.

When she was inducted into the Phi Beta Kappa honor society in college, their keynote speaker explained that many women feel ashamed and undeserving of recognition instead of believing they're worthy of it. Regardless of their expertise in their chosen fields or having great accomplishments, they feel like impostors with insufficient skills and abilities.

This circumstance where competent people are haunted by a sense of self-doubt is called the impostor syndrome. Everyone is prone to it, but women are more likely to face it and be restrained by it.

When women feel as if they're a fraud, it's a sign of a much greater problem. They are constantly underestimating themselves. In fact, studies found that women frequently believe their job performance was worse than it really was, while men believe they performed a lot better than they really did.

In terms of success, men acknowledge their own natural skills and qualities, while women credit their success to external factors, saying they worked hard, they simply got lucky, or they had support from others. When it comes to failure, men simply say they didn't study hard enough or the topic wasn't interesting for them, while women believe it's because they lack a certain ability. Even media and colleagues give credit for women's accomplishments to external factors. This, in turn, breeds insecurity, which harms future performance.

It wasn't until Sheryl heard the speech in college regarding self-doubt that she realized the real problem was not feeling like an impostor but that she could feel something deeply and profoundly and be totally wrong. When she thought of her brother, raised the same way she was but possessing far more confidence, she realized women are the ones who typically doubt themselves.

Her experiences taught her that she needed to make certain improvements both intellectually and emotionally. While it can be quite difficult to get rid of self-doubt, she could object to the idea of always heading for failure.

We all have met or know overconfident people who don't deserve to feel that way as well as people who are capable of doing more if they just learned to believe in themselves. People who think they will fail are really doomed to failure.

Whenever you're not feeling optimistic, faking it can sometimes help. In fact, the strategy of faking it is backed up by research. A study shows that when people take on a high-power position for a few minutes, the levels of dominance hormone rise and the levels of stress hormone decrease. This makes them feel more in control and powerful, and they can tolerate greater risk. By simply changing their posture, they are significantly changing their attitude.

Confidence is essential to get more opportunities. Since opportunities aren't always offered, you must grab them. When Sheryl was working at Google, she noticed that men were reaching for opportunities faster than women. They were also quicker to pursue opportunities for growth and believed they could do more. The women were more careful in terms of changing roles and searching for new challenges.

In this fast-paced world, it's really important to grab opportunities. When someone jumps on an opportunity, that opportunity can eventually become his job. You don't just sit and wait for someone to tell you what you should do. You have to keep on grabbing opportunities. The ability to learn and contribute is what matters. Being able to learn is an important trait a leader must have.

Women not only fail to lead, but they also fail to take note and correct this gap. When Sheryl gave a talk about gender issues at Facebook, a woman approached her later that day to tell Sheryl that she had learned to keep her hand raised. She explained that when Sheryl had announced she was almost done taking questions at her talk, women immediately put their hands down while men kept their hands raised, and Sheryl continued answering their questions. People and institutions need to see and correct this behavior by promoting, encouraging, and supporting more women. Women also need to keep raising their hands so other people will start noticing.

It's important for both men and women to recognize success and thank the people who offered help and gave their support along the way. No one succeeds alone. Even Sheryl believes that she needs to trust her own skills to grow.

3: Success and Likeability

In 2003, two professors conducted an investigation to examine men's and women's judgments within the workplace. It was a case study regarding the life of Heidi Roizen, a real-life entrepreneur. A section of students was assigned to look through Heidi's story, while the other section was given the very same story, except the professors changed the name to Howard.

The students admired both individuals, but Howard seemed to be a more desirable colleague. Heidi was regarded as self-centered and not the kind of person someone would work for or even employ. Similar data with gender differences produce immensely contrasting perceptions.

This investigation shows that men and women like a man who is successful. On the other hand, they dislike a woman who is successful. While nobody truly admits to stereotyping based on gender, we obviously do. Because we separate men from women, professional accomplishment and all its attributes are mostly given to the males.

This prejudice explains why most women are held back and also why they hold themselves back. For women, professional success is often considered unfavorably. When a woman does great at her work, her coworkers tend to like her less. They think she's too aggressive, political, difficult, or she doesn't work well with a team.

Surely, we notice this punishment for achieving success. We know all too well that women can be strong and competitive. However, society doesn't expect them to behave like this. A woman who gets her job done or is highly competent is viewed as manly, which makes people dislike her. As a result, women tend to hide their professional achievements due to the negative reactions directed at them. In order to protect themselves from being disliked by others, they question their abilities and downplay their achievements. They put themselves down before others can.

For Sheryl, throughout her life, culturally promoted signs warned her against being labeled as too successful or too smart. As a girl, being smart is good in many ways, but it doesn't make you especially popular or appealing to boys. Sheryl went to great efforts to stifle her achievements at a young age. Our established cultural ideals associate men with leadership qualities and women with nurturing qualities and that women should be solely nurturing.

A competent woman is not considered nice enough. If a

woman is nice, she's not really considered competent. This creates a real struggle for women since people want to employ and promote those who are both nice and competent. It makes it difficult for women to reach for the same opportunities as men, but going against expectations and reaching for those opportunities leads to being judged as undeserving and selfish.

Most people want to be liked. It's actually an important factor in both personal and professional success. We need to believe that women are capable of doing their jobs and that they can get along with others quite well at the same time.

Feeling confident in your own success is the key to attaining more success. Professional advancement depends upon people believing that the efforts of an employee are yielding great results. Men can comfortably claim credit for the things they do, as long as they don't appear too arrogant. For women, recognizing their own success might only attract negative remarks.

When it comes to negotiations, people expect men to promote themselves, highlight their contributions, and anticipate rewards and recognition. However, people react unfavorably when women endorse themselves or point out their own value. They are seen as more demanding.

A successful negotiation aims to achieve certain objectives while continuing to have people like us. According to a professor who studies gender and negotiations, women can boost their chances of achieving the desired outcome if they appear nice, concerned about others, suitably female, and also provide a reasonable explanation for the negotiation.

Telling a current employer about an offer from another company is a common method that easily works for men. Men are allowed to center on their own achievements, while women are only expected to be loyal. It isn't surprising why women don't negotiate as often as men. Women can participate in certain negotiations while keeping in mind that when they show concern for the good of others, even if they're negotiating for themselves, they can strengthen their position.

Also, learning to withstand criticism is important for women. Ariana Huffington, the founder of *The Huffington Post*, suggests that women should let themselves react emotionally and feel whatever criticism stimulates in them. And then they should immediately move on. She sees children as her role model because children are capable of crying one moment and running off to play the next.

In addition, we can all benefit from acknowledging shared efforts. Well-functioning groups are much stronger than individuals. Teams that work well together outperform those that don't. Success truly feels a lot better when you have others with whom you can celebrate.

4: It's a Jungle Gym, Not a Ladder

Throughout her career, Sheryl hired thousands of people. She observed that people usually concentrate on finding the appropriate role for themselves, implying that their skills will help the company. It wasn't until after she got a call from someone looking for a job who asked what Facebook's biggest problem was and how they could help solve it that she began to think about this exceptional approach.

People often compare their careers to a ladder. However, this idea no longer works for most people. Today, average Americans from the ages of eighteen to forty-six have already had eleven jobs. People are no longer entering a corporation or organization just to stay there and climb a ladder. Careers are now described as a jungle gym instead.

People are restrained by ladders. They aren't given enough options as to where they could possibly go with their potential. Jungle gyms provide a more innovative journey. Also, a ladder only gives you one option – to reach the top – while a jungle gym offers plenty of ways to reach your goal. It's a model that benefits everyone. It presents a better chance for fulfillment.

For Sheryl, this best describes her career. When people ask her how she plotted her course, she usually tells them she actually didn't. That surprises them and relieves them at the same time. It seems reassuring for people, knowing that careers don't really need to be completely laid out from the beginning.

Throughout her childhood, Sheryl's parents emphasized that it's important to search for a meaningful life. At the dinner table, they often talked about social injustice and the people who fight to create a better world. As a child, Sheryl never thought about what she wanted to be, although she thought a lot about what she wanted to do. She hoped to change the world. While she doesn't believe in making plans for every step of your career, she does believe it would help if you have a long-term dream or goal.

It doesn't matter whether your long-term dream is specific or realistic. It may express your desire to travel around the world or work in a specific field. Still, even if your goal seems vague, it can give you a direction.

The first job she took was at the World Bank as a research assistant and later joined a health field mission to India to learn more of the Bank's true mission, which is to lessen global poverty. Her team worked toward eliminating leprosy, which was endemic in the most distant and poorest regions of India.

Upon returning, she was planning to attend law school, but an economist at the World Bank persuaded her to enter business school instead because he felt that would be a better option for her. After attending business school, she eventually served as a special assistant to the deputy secretary of the Treasury Department. During those years, she watched the first technology boom thrive from a distance. Its impact was evident and appealing. Technology was changing communication and transforming lives everywhere. Her long-term dream instinct kicked in, and when President Clinton's administration ended and she found herself out of a job, she moved to Silicon Valley.

After some time searching for employment, Google's founders offered her a job. However, after comparing it with her other options, the job they offered wasn't completely clear to her. Eric Schmidt, Google's CEO whom she had met several times when she worked at the Treasury, then explained to her the only thing that matters when choosing a job is fast growth. Eric told her, "If you're offered a seat on a rocket ship, you don't ask what seat. You just get on." In that moment, Sheryl made up her mind. Even though Google was small and disorganized, it had a mission she deeply believed in. She took the job.

In any field, there exist jobs that offer more growth potential than others. People in older industries can search for rocket ships – departments or units that are expanding – inside their workplace. In careers like teaching or medicine, people can find positions where their skills are in higher demand.

Sheryl also believes in having an eighteen-month plan, since two years feels too long and a year feels too short, although an exact amount of time doesn't really matter. First, she sets goals for what her team can achieve. Employees who focus on results and significance are considered extremely valuable. It's just good business. Second, she tries to set more personal goals and see how she can improve in the following months. Everyone has plenty of room to grow.

In her professional life, she has learned to accept uncertainty and fully welcome it. It's what landed her at Google. Since it worked so well for her, she decided to embrace risk again, which led her to Facebook. She learned to prioritize potential for fast growth and the company's mission above title.

People tend to miss a lot of great opportunities because they focus too much on their career status. Women need to open up and take risks in their careers. If you want to become a leader, you must seek out various experiences. Take risks, choose growth, challenge yourself, and ask for promotions. These are all necessary for managing a career. Don't wait for others to offer you power. Seize it. Otherwise, it might never show up.

5: Are You My Mentor?

Every time Sheryl gives speeches or sits at meetings, women introduce themselves to her and ask her if she could be their mentor. She can't think of any man asking her for that same guidance. While this can be flattering, it can also be uncomfortable.

For the past several years, the subject of mentorship or sponsorship has been the number one topic at any women's career seminar. It's the focus of newspaper articles, research reports, and blogs. Many young women respond to frequently repeated advice telling them that in order to climb the corporate ladder, they need mentors and sponsors.

The value of seeking out a mentor became particularly clear to Sheryl when she was invited to speak at Harvard Business School. The men's questions centered on managing a business, while the women focused on maintaining a career. While the men were seeking answers, the women were seeking guidance and permission. It seems that women are often taught to depend too much on others.

Clearly, mentorship is necessary. Sponsorship and mentorship are essential for career advancement. Unfortunately, it's easier for men to acquire and maintain these relationships. Studies also show that men are sponsored a lot a more, and those who have sponsors find a sense of satisfaction in terms of their levels of advancement.

Since it's difficult for women to get mentored and sponsored, they tend to become more active in finding people to guide them. The truth is, a strong relationship comes from a real and deserved connection, which both sides usually feel.

Sheryl has been fortunate to be guided and supported throughout her career. Influential people have encouraged her, introduced her, and been good examples to her. Their wisdom and guidance helped her avoid mistakes and clean up any messes she wasn't smart enough to avoid. In turn, she has tried to offer guidance to others.

Studies have found that mentors choose students based on their performance and capacity. Mentors devote their time to mentees who are sincerely open to criticism and manage their time effectively.

Keep in mind that it's also important to prepare when searching for a job. The things you want to do must be clear enough to you before you go marching in front of people who can possibly hire you. This way, you'll be able to talk about specific opportunities they could give you.

Mentorship is actually a reciprocal relationship. Even if the mentee receives direct assistance, the mentor benefits as well. He can have a greater commitment from his associates, obtain useful information, and a feeling of pride and fulfillment. Everybody flourishes when mentoring is done the right way.

There are other ways to find a mentor than simply grabbing the attention of a senior executive with a stellar performance. There are junior employees who grab a moment in the hall or after a meeting to ask advice from a respected superior. It's usually just a quick and casual exchange. After taking the advice, the junior person does a follow up to convey his gratitude and grabs the opportunity to seek more advice. The senior person eventually becomes vested in the career of the junior person.

Mentors also have to deal with their extremely stressful jobs. Instead of complaining to them, it's always better for mentees to center the discussion on particular problems with actual solutions. For high-potential women, it's hard to ask people for help because they don't want to appear lacking. Asking for opinions is not a sign of weakness but often the first step to finding a path forward.

Mentoring or sponsoring relationships usually form between people with common interests or when a senior person sees himself in the junior member. Since there are fewer women in high positions, it's almost impossible for junior women to receive adequate support unless men start jumping in, too. If male leaders wish to move towards an equal world, they can prioritize this issue and become part of the solution.

Lower-ranking women and superior men frequently avoid mentorship or sponsorship relationships because they're afraid of what other people might think. We must put an end to this kind of evasiveness. Personal connections open doors for appointments and promotions, which is why men and women must feel that it's okay for them to come together, just like men do with each other. Everyone must behave appropriately so men and women feel safe anywhere.

Many companies are now coming up with formal programs to provide help and guidance for their employees. A study even shows that women received more chances of promotion when they were mentored by means of these formal programs.

You can seek counsel from anyone. In fact, your peers can also serve as your mentor or sponsor. They may actually offer more immediate and beneficial guidance. Peers may even understand problems that your superiors don't.

6: Seek and Speak Your Truth

When we attempt to speak appropriately, somehow, we tend to lose authenticity. Authentic communication isn't always easy. However, it's important if we want to achieve real efficiency at work and form great relationships in our homes. People have a habit of avoiding honesty to defend others or protect themselves, which causes numerous problems. We must learn to be brave enough to speak the truth.

It's difficult to be honest at work. Almost all companies consist of hierarchy, and an individual's performance is often assessed by other people's perceptions. Psychologists who study power dynamics found that people in lower positions tend to be more hesitant in sharing their views, and they often limit the things they say. This explains why many women are afraid of speaking honestly in their workplace. They worry that people won't consider them a team player, that they'll appear negative or nagging, or that by speaking up, they'll call attention to themselves.

Combining authenticity and appropriateness results in better communication, where opinions are delicately rather than brutally honest. While it's easy for some to tell the truth without hurting someone's feelings, others have to work at it.

Sheryl learned that effective communication begins by understanding that there are different points of view. There is no absolute truth. People who think they're speaking the truth may only be silencing others. When we understand that we see things from our own perspective, it will be easier for us to share our ideas cautiously.

It also helps to convey the truth using simple language, especially if it's a hard truth. Many organizations can perform better if people are clear with their statements.

Listening is as important as speaking. Understanding the other person's viewpoint clears up conflict and leads to resolution. We all want to be heard, and we become better listeners when we show to others that we are listening.

The first step to solving a problem is being aware of the problem. It's difficult to tell how others perceive our actions. We can try to guess, but it's more effective to ask directly. When we have concrete knowledge, we can easily change our actions.

Having an honest conversation regarding business decisions is difficult, but it's even more difficult to give people honest feedback. It helps to remember that, much like the truth, feedback is not absolute. It's simply an opinion that stems from experiences and observations. It lets us know what impression we make on others. Yet, the information is revealing and often uncomfortable, which is why we'd rather give feedback to those who want it.

Asking for advice can help form relationships. Sheryl learned the hard way that being open to finding out the truth means taking responsibility for your mistakes, and she took the wrong step of starting a working relationship during her first week as chief of staff at Treasury.

Another way for Sheryl to try to stimulate authentic communication is to speak openly about her own weaknesses, like getting impatient about unresolved situations. She acknowledged her impatience openly and asked her colleagues to let her know when she needs to loosen up. If she had never said anything, she doubts they would say a word to her. When you recognize people's honesty in public, it encourages them to keep being honest while sending a strong message to others.

Another tool people use to deliver an honest message in a pleasant way is by using humor. Studies say that people who are regarded as effective leaders often have a sense of humor.

Unfortunately, there are times when our sense of humor fails to save us in desperate situations. Research shows that women believe it's not okay to cry at work. But the truth is, when you share emotions, you form deeper relationships. Motivation comes from working on things we care about and with the people we care about. Emotion drives both men and women and influences every decision we make. Being able to talk about emotions makes us better partners, managers, and peers.

Being professional doesn't always mean being organized, focused, and keeping your personal life separate. An all-business approach isn't always good business. Sometimes, you need to take a moment to connect with people before diving in.

Sheryl truly believes in bringing our entire selves to work. When we express our truth, talk about personal circumstances, and accept that emotions often drive professional decisions, we can benefit greatly. True leaders express their honesty through their personalities. Rather than aiming for perfection, leaders should strive for authenticity.

7: Don't Leave Before You Leave

At a young age, girls are given the idea they'll eventually have to decide on whether to go after a successful job or become a good mother. Once they enter college, women begin to stress themselves out, thinking they might have to trade their professional life for personal goals or vice versa.

Although Sheryl truly believes in thoughtful preparation, planning too far ahead when it comes to combining career and family can shut doors rather than open them. There are many ways in which women limit themselves, but it seems the most prevalent one is that they're instantly looking for the exit.

This is how the scenario takes place. An ambitious and successful woman travels down a difficult career path, keeping in mind that she wants to have children someday. Once she has found the right partner, the thought of having children immediately tops everything else in her mind. She thinks that the only way to support a child is for her to step back from her job. She doesn't realize that she already stopped searching for more opportunities.

Earlier in her professional life, she excels greatly, handling equal responsibilities, given good opportunities and pay.

119

However, she starts falling behind because she didn't search for ways to expand herself throughout the years that lead to motherhood. The moment she goes back to her workplace after giving birth, she tends to feel unfulfilled, undervalued, or underutilized. She might even lower her ambitions even more because she gave up on the hopes of getting to a high point in her career. Moreover, if she has enough resources to quit her job, she probably will.

There's a lower chance for a person to leave the workplace if she appears to be satisfied with her job. The sad thing is that women end up leaving their jobs because of everything they have done to stay on their job. They are stuck in a career that's less fulfilling and less engaging.

People have different reasons for leaving the workforce. Oftentimes, the right choice for them is to become a full-time parent at home, which is a great thing. People shouldn't judge others based on their personal decisions. Dedicating one's life to raising the next generation is altogether important, demanding, and joyful work.

The only time you should consider scaling back is when you need a break or when your child arrives. Women shouldn't step back before they even have a child, and certainly not years in advance. It's important for women to lean in, especially during the time that leads up to them having children.

Years ago, Sheryl started tackling this subject directly. She made it clear that she's only addressing the issue and asking questions to make sure that her women employees aren't limiting their options unnecessarily. Still, Sheryl doesn't recommend that every woman put herself forward regardless of the circumstances because there were plenty of times when she herself preferred not to.

For some women, pregnancy allows them to stay focused and provides them a set deadline to work towards. The advent of a child can instantly change how we define ourselves. Women turn into mothers, and men turn into fathers. Couples become parents. Our priorities change in crucial ways. Although parenting is considered the most rewarding experience, it's also the hardest and most humbling.

New parents usually face the question of who will primarily take care of the child. The mother has always been the choice since breastfeeding made her the logical and biological choice. But the development of the modern-day breast pump has changed the situation. Despite that, women still provide the majority of childcare. As a result, women's participation in the workforce decreases when they become a parent.

Women who typically drop out of the workforce are either married to the highest-earning men or the lowest-earning men. Mothers married to the lowest-earning men struggle to look for jobs with sufficient pay to cover their needed expenses. Women married to the highest-earning men are more likely to leave due to the excessive number of hours that their husbands worked. Many of the women who leave their jobs are those with the highest levels of education, widening the gap in terms of leadership.

It's easy to anticipate society's response when someone becomes a parent. The widely held assumption is that raising a child is a woman's responsibility. Women who can afford to leave their workplace usually get both permission and encouragement to go for it from every direction. If society truly values the work of raising children, companies and institutions would find ways to lessen these unreasonable punishments and support parents in combining their career and family responsibilities.

Anyone fortunate enough to be given options should keep them open. Don't enter the workforce and then look for the exit right away. Go up. Just keep moving forward until you get to the time where you have to make a real decision.

8: Make Your Partner a Real Partner

For Sheryl, motherhood brought her a lot of amazing experiences. However, giving birth was extremely difficult, so much so that during labor, she injured her leg and was on crutches for a week after leaving the hospital. Usually, it's the mother who takes care of the new baby, but because of her injury, it was her husband who primarily took care of their newborn. Sheryl's husband actually taught her how to change diapers when their son was eight days old. They hadn't planned that role reversal and joked that if they had, they would have been geniuses.

An interview with a Ph.D. candidate regarding working couples overwhelmed her and made her realize that she and her husband weren't truly prepared to deal with certain responsibilities. They had spent plenty of time talking about how they would do things, but it was all in the abstract. Although they often discussed parenthood, they didn't talk about the practical things. Their inexperience made it even harder for them to know how to cover the specifics. They had very little idea of what they were facing.

They were also in denial of the tremendous change that would be happening in their lives, which was fast approaching. They weren't even working in the same city

123

when Sheryl got pregnant. She was in northern California, while her husband was in Los Angeles. They decided to settle in the Bay Area to have a life together. They had a certain pattern of doing things that continued after their marriage.

Still, her husband wasn't around all the time, so the major task of taking care of the child fell to Sheryl. She eventually felt they had an uneven division of labor, and it was hurting their marriage. Even with the help of a nanny, their problems couldn't be solved. In just a short amount of time, they had fallen into the traditional and unequal gender roles.

Even public policy promotes gender bias. According to the U.S. Census Bureau, mothers are considered the assigned parent inside the home even when both parents are present. Some men even feel like they're babysitting when they're watching over their own children.

Nevertheless, while mothers seem more likely to be nurturing, fathers are capable of matching the same skills with effort and knowledge. We must challenge the common assumptions if we wish to see more women succeed at work and more men succeed at home. Both men and women must be empowered at work and at home.

We don't always have to follow biology. It simply requires the willingness of the mother or the father to make a difference. We overcome biology with consciousness in other areas. We try to use willpower to go against biology. It simply requires a willing mother and a willing father. It doesn't always have to be the mother who remembers what to put in their child's lunch box.

Finding a genuine partner doesn't have to be a rare occurrence. It's typical for women to be viewed as nurturing, but we don't really expect men to be the same. Anyone who wishes to have a real partner needs to treat him as though he is equally capable. If they want to share responsibilities, they must truly share responsibilities. Each partner needs to be in charge of specific activities. Otherwise, one would have a tendency to feel as if he's doing his partner a favor, rather than offering to do his part. A lot of things can change in positive ways if partners learn to share the burden of accomplishing tedious tasks.

Sheryl believes that choosing to have a partner in life or who that might be is the most important decision a woman has to make. Contrary to what our society thinks, many successful women in business who are taking on leadership roles have life partners who constantly support them in their career.

Studies have found that children gain benefits from having a loving and involved father at home. Their psychological well-being is higher, they have greater educational achievements, better mental skills, lower rates of misconduct, and they are socially competent and more empathetic.

Unfortunately, fathers don't take a lot of time off work for their new child. Men who wish to completely resign from their jobs to dedicate their lives to taking care of their children also face a great deal of negative societal pressure.

It's a punishment for women when society believes they are more devoted to their family over their jobs. Employers assume they are not dedicated enough when seeking professional jobs. On the other hand, society expects men to prioritize their career over their personal achievements, which makes them feel less valued or fulfilled.

If you want to find the right partner, make sure that you both seek an equal partnership. Find someone who supports women who are smart, ambitious, and opinionated. Look for someone who gives importance to fairness and is willing to do his part inside the home. Good men still exist.

Equality between partners leads to happier relationships. Having true partnership also sets a good example for future generations. Women need to pursue what they want for their careers, while men need to strive to do well inside the home.

9: The Myth of Doing It All

The belief that someone can have it all sets a trap for many women. No one can really have everything despite everything we have or how much we appreciate every single thing. We all deal with the limited resources of life, and we try our best to give equal time to our relationships, career, and family.

The idea of having everything is a myth, although it can send a helpful cautionary message. Choosing to have both a personal and professional life is attainable and even noble. Women should learn to aim for the sky, but they also need to remember that we all have limits.

In addition, nobody can do everything. We all have constant decisions to make. For some people, sacrificing and experiencing hardships are necessary in life. Mothers who are working in professional settings are always reminded of different challenges they have to face. Working parents struggle with several responsibilities. Still, mothers are the ones who need to tolerate the accusatory looks and the insulting questions thrown at them that make them think they're failing at their jobs and in their homes.

Trying so hard to do everything and expecting to do

everything perfectly only leads to disappointment. The secret is to learn where to direct your attention. We all have limited patience and time. And no matter how much you try to prepare in life, the struggles of parenthood just keep on coming.

You can't control every factor in terms of parenting. For women who are used to success in business by planning ahead and pushing themselves toward their goals, it may be particularly distressing for them to combine the orderliness of their career with the chaos of motherhood. It's always better to get things done than to do things perfectly. Aiming for perfection can be frustrating and paralyzing.

Sometimes attaining success, in the long run, depends on whether we try to fulfill every demand made of us. You have to make deliberate choices, set some limits, and comply with them so it will be easier for you to manage both your career and personal life. You have to focus on the things that really matter.

Sheryl understood the fear women have in terms of looking like they're putting their families first before their careers. Working mothers want to avoid other people thinking they are not entirely dedicated to their jobs. Even when people are offered flexibility at work, they're afraid it will harm their career and their peers will see them as less devoted. All of these things need to change, especially since recent evidence suggests people who are working from home seem to be a lot more productive.

Technology is also affecting the importance of sticking to office hours since everyone can keep doing their work online. While technology sets us free from the workplace, it also prolongs the workday. Nevertheless, employees are still judged by their physical presence at the office rather than their output. As a result, many employees become too focused on their working hours instead of accomplishing their goals effectively. The truth is, if both companies and individuals pay more attention to the outcomes, then it will turn out to be beneficial for all.

The new norm establishes that twenty-four hours aren't enough for a day. Even people without children are overworked. However, sleeping for only four or five hours a night leads to mental impairment. It's like driving a car with alcohol in your system. Sleep deprivation makes people anxious, irritable, and confused.

Just as in the workplace, the home has formed a new kind of normal as well. A current working mother spends about the same amount of time taking care of the family as a nonemployed mother back in 1975. Employed mothers are constantly being judged; even if they spend plenty of time taking care of their children, they still feel like they're failing.

Studies have found it's not evidence but rather emotion that is the basis for the pressure society places on women that makes them choose to stay at home and do what's necessary for their children. However, it's important to acknowledge that even if parents choose to work outside their home, they are still capable of providing their children with a secure and loving home.

Setting attainable goals is the way to obtain happiness. Instead of aiming for perfection, we should strive for sustainable and fulfilling. Success is being able to make the best choices and completely accept them. Do the best you can with what you've got.

10: Let's Start Talking About It

No individual wants others to think of them as weak, which is why a lot of women dismiss gender identification. No one wants to limit her achievements. Yet, the world has a way of reminding them that women are women, and girls are girls.

When Sheryl was in college, she believed the world no longer needed feminists. She and her friends mistakenly thought there was nothing left to fight for. Upon entering the workforce, she figured that if sexism still existed, she would just prove it wrong. She would do her job and do it well. What she didn't know at the time was that ignoring the issue is a standard method of survival. Within traditional institutions, a woman's success depends upon not speaking out but simply fitting in.

Early in her career, her gender was rarely noted, and everything was completely fine. Women were fitting in, and they had no reason to call any attention to themselves. But while gender was not openly acknowledged, it was still hiding underneath the surface. She started noticing how often employees were judged not by their real performance but by how well they fit in.

When Sheryl was invited to speak at the Women's Media Center in New York, she began her talk by explaining that women were taught to fit in when it comes to business but that she was starting to believe that might not be the right way. Men and women differ in behavior, and there's a difference in the way others consider their behavior. We need to be able to talk about gender without people thinking that women are only crying for help or asking for special treatment.

We need to break off the status quo. Staying quiet and fitting in may have been all the first generations of women could do upon entering corporate America. In certain circumstances, it might still be the safest way. However, this strategy is not paying off for women as a group. Women need to speak out, identify the barriers holding them back, and find solutions.

Many things can change through several encouraging techniques or small interventions. They can push people to act in various ways during crucial moments. Simply talking about these patterns of behavior makes people become aware of the issue. Talking can change minds, which leads to changes in behavior and institutions.

It isn't easy. The topic itself expresses a contradiction. It causes us to accept our differences even as we seek to be treated equally. Women are worried that they will appear unprofessional or that it will seem they're blaming others when raising gender issues. They're afraid that if they speak up, the situation will only get worse, or they'll end up being punished or fired.

Shutting down discussion only hinders progress. Since the majority of managers are men, they need to feel comfortable addressing these issues directly with their female employees.

One obstacle is that many people think the workplace is a political orientation. We see individuals rather than groups and determine different outcomes based on merit, not gender. Men with power can be blind to the disadvantages associated with being a woman. Women also believe that men at the top deserve to be there, so they try to keep up with the rules and work harder to advance. Everyone ends up upholding an unjust system.

Gender doesn't have to be instilled into every discussion. Today, mentioning gender in work situations often makes people visibly uncomfortable. Many institutions have worked hard to sensitize people to these issues, but they have also raised the prospects of legal action, which can create real barriers to these conversations. It's worth some serious attention so we can deal with these issues in a way that protects but doesn't suppress.

Gender bias exists. Our preconceived ideas about both genders affect the way we judge and interact with our colleagues at work. Thinking that we are objective can actually make things worse, creating a so-called "bias blind spot." It causes people to become so confident about their own powers of objectivity that they fail to correct for bias.

The goal is to give women something men tend to receive automatically, which is the benefit of the doubt. Women shouldn't be afraid to ask, even if it seems like a long shot. Being direct and honest can lead to opportunity.

Most jobs will entail some sacrifices. You just need to avoid making pointless sacrifices, and that will be difficult since our culture gives high regard to absolute commitment. We have a long way to go before flex time is accepted in most workplaces. It will only happen if we keep raising the issue. The discussions may be difficult, but there are plenty of benefits that will come from it. We can't change what we are unaware of, but once we recognize the problems, we can't resist change.

Social rewards must be seized. Leaders of the women's movement spoke out loudly and bravely to demand the rights that women now have. Creating an equal environment will not only result in better performance for our institutions but also greater happiness for all.

11: Working Together Toward Equality

Women today are far stronger and wiser than before. Still, the purpose of real equality continues to evade us. True equality can only be achieved when more women strive to be at the top of governments and industries. We all need to work hard to get there. Our differences must be accepted rather than disregarded. It's how we can go beyond them.

For many years, we tried to give women the right to choose to work outside or inside the home. However, we constantly failed to motivate them to seek out leadership positions. We must inspire every girl and every woman who wants to sit at the table to look for new challenges and grow in her career.

Today, even though we have accomplished many things, men and women still don't have real choices. Equal opportunity can only be equal once everyone is encouraged to seize every opportunity laid out in front of them. This is how both men and women can achieve their highest potential.

This will only be possible if we all work towards the same goals together. Men must support women, and women must support other women as well. If we learn to stand alongside each other, everything will be better.

Oftentimes, women in higher positions receive greater scrutiny. Since most leaders are men, we can't generalize from any one source. However, because there are only a few female leaders, one woman seems to represent her whole gender. While it is completely unfair for the individual, it also strengthens the idea that women who are successful are unlikeable.

We should aim to settle our differences right away. When we don't agree with others, we must remember to focus on our common goals. This isn't a way to avoid debate but a way to have a more constructive discussion.

It's sad to admit, but sometimes women are not allowed the chance to gain power because of other women who are already in authority. Instead of going hand-in-hand to stand against an unjust system, women often think they are competing with one another.

While it no longer makes sense for women to become rivals, some still end up competing against each other. When a woman holds another woman back, it's nothing but tragic. The consequences go beyond solitary pain. Women don't realize they're only echoing unappreciative cultural attitudes. In the end, women don't just become the victims of gender bias; they also become the guilty party.

There's still hope that things can change. In fact, a survey shows that women who work in business are reaching out to help other women develop their skills and talents. If more women continue to help each other, then we can further help ourselves. If we work together, we can produce positive results. This also includes men who truly care about achieving equality. Gender shouldn't be an excuse to treat others dismissively or negatively. We must expect professional behavior and show kindness to one another.

If men want to help change the leadership percentage, they can do so by actively seeking qualified female candidates to hire or promote, or start mentoring, sponsoring, and recruiting women so they can obtain the needed experience.

Women have been working throughout their lives to make sure they're not failing those who made it possible for them to go after their ambitions. Feminism was meant for people to be free and capable of making choices without any guilt.

Society has been downgrading the contributions of people who aren't paid for their work. All we want is to feel comfortable and contented with the decisions we make and to be understood by everyone around us. We should aim to support one another.

We can only achieve true equality when we put an end to the

stereotypes that prevent us from developing our potential. We should utilize our energy to break this cycle. Our goal is to create a world where there are no social norms to rule our lives, a world where we are simply expected to share our talents, passions, and interests.

Conclusion

It's time to put an end to the notion that women can't do what men can. If we truly look forward to having a better and equal world, then there's no excuse for not promoting ways to empower women. Believing that things can be done assures that things will be done.

Women should not be afraid to aspire to leadership roles. If given equal chances, they can certainly prove they have the same skills needed to lead as men. They must be welcomed to sit at the table because women's voices are essential if it's truly in our good intentions to consider what's best for everyone.

Rather than putting negative labels on someone based on gender, we must learn to appreciate his or her accomplishments because, in the end, a person's contributions are what benefits us all. It shouldn't matter which gender gets to the top. The ability to help make a difference to create a better world should be our top priority.

Success is not a one-way street. Women should not be limited by the things society thinks they should do. Like men, they have the right to take charge, and whether we admit it or not, some women even deserve to lead more than some men.

In order to become true leaders, sometimes we must strive to have authentic communication with one another more than perfection. This way, women would have the courage not to silence themselves or hold themselves back. Men need to encourage and support more women to achieve true success.

Being a mother shouldn't strip any opportunities from women. In fact, it's a good reason for women to grab opportunities and not leave the workforce if they don't want to. If men can work professionally and help manage their homes at the same time, so can women. If women choose to keep their careers, that doesn't mean they're neglecting their families. It would be better if husbands contributed more in the home so wives can reach for more opportunities outside the home. Taking care of the household is also real and hard work. It is a shared responsibility for both parents.

Women should keep fighting for their rightful place in the world, and men should stop ignoring them if they truly value equality. Everyone should be working together towards greater success.

Hopefully, this book inspires women to chase their dreams, form a path in spite of the hurdles, and reach their maximum potential. Exploiting the abilities of every individual will surely lead to more productive organizations and happier homes. There are no more reasons for children to be held back by stereotypes.

If women continue to lean in, opportunities will expand for all. Equality will exist. We can finally bridge the gap in terms of leadership. Every person's success can make things easier and simpler for the generations to come. Soon enough, we won't need male or female leaders, only leaders.

The moment women lead more in the workplace and men contribute more in the home, there's no doubt that this world will become a whole lot better.

FREE BONUSES

P.S. Is it okay if we overdeliver?

Here at Readtrepreneur Publishing, we believe in overdelivering way beyond our reader's expectations. Is it okay if we overdeliver?

Here's the deal, we're going to give you an extremely condensed PDF summary of the book which you've just read and much more...

What's the catch? We need to trust you... You see, we want to overdeliver and in order for us to do that, we've to trust our reader to keep this bonus a secret to themselves? Why? Because we don't want people to be getting our exclusive PDF summaries even without buying our books itself. Unethical, right?

Ok. Are you ready?

Firstly, remember that your book is code: "**READ50**".

Next, visit this link: **http://bit.ly/exclusivepdfs**

Everything else will be self explanatory after you've visited: **http://bit.ly/exclusivepdfs.**

We hope you'll enjoy our free bonuses as much as we enjoyed preparing it for you!